How to Learn to Dance in Colombia

Neil Bennion

HOW TO LEARN TO DANCE IN COLOMBIA

Enquiries: contact@neilbennion.com

Contents

Maps

Introduction   1

Why Learn to Dance?   2

Why Dance with a Partner?   3

Why Learn on your Travels?   4

Why Learn in Colombia?   6

Colombia's Dance Culture   7

Is Colombia Safe?   8

A Quick History Lesson   11

An Even Quicker Geography Lesson   13

Colombia's Musical Geography   14

Which City?   17

Which Dance?   23

Dance Class Specifics   26

How to Recognise the Music   33

Finding Schools   36

Choosing a School   39

Dance Classes in Detail   42

Mind Management   45

Leading and Following   47

The Language Barrier   49

Proximity and Boundaries   51

Practice   54

Remembering Dance Moves   57

Finding a Dance Partner   60

What to Wear   63

Putting it Out There   65

Drinking and Dancing   68

Dance and Romance   69

Etiquette   72

Overcoming Fear   76

Over to You   77

Miscellaneous

Maps

Introduction

My name is Neil Bennion and I'm a writer from England. Motivated by a desire to address my lifelong rubbishness at dancing, I went to Colombia for six or seven months to learn to dance like a Colombian. I tried all the major urban dances, and even tried my hand at a few folk dances, for the purposes of fun and ritual self-humiliation. In total I learnt something like nine different dances to one standard or another, so I have a familiarity with the common problems faced by learners, especially dance-floor cowards like myself.

You can read all about my adventures in the book Dancing Feat: One Man's Mission to Dance Like a Colombian.

During my time in Colombia, I found that the information for a foreigner wanting to learn how to dance was quite patchy. Not only that but the whole world of dance in general was somewhat impenetrable for an outsider. How do you find a dance school? How about a partner? What do you wear? How do you ask somebody to dance? And what the heck is this music?

I learned the answers to all these questions the hard way, over many months. Hopefully by reading this book, your path will be a little easier.

My own viewpoint of dancing is, by its nature, male-orientated, so I've invited Colombian journalist Vanessa Ruggiero for some female insights, which I'll include where relevant. I've also included here the history and geography sections from my book 47 Amazing Things to See and Do in Colombia, as they offer a good primer.

Anyway, let's get on with it.

Why Learn to Dance?

There are so many reasons why you should learn to dance.

Firstly, it's a whole lot of fun, especially if you know what you're doing. It can also be something that is fulfilling in a much deeper way as you progress and improve over a period of time. Indeed, it's a great activity for getting into the state of 'flow' — a mentally absorbed (and psychologically beneficial) state which occurs when you're performing a complicated task, but one that you're skilled at. Most people recognise it as that sense of being 'in the zone'.

On top of that, it's great exercise, and all the more so because it's enjoyable. You're so consumed in the activity, that you accrue the physical benefits without thinking about it. Do it for long enough and it will improve not just the condition of your body, but also your stature and even the way you carry yourself when you move.

Furthermore, dance is also a wonderful channel for self-expression. If you're someone who really 'feels' music and are frustrated that you can't express yourself better to it, then being able to dance will allow you to do that. Of course if you're a miserable sod and like depressing music, then arguably this might just translate to the same thing on the dance floor. But at least you'll be able to express your miserable sod-ness via one more medium than you used to.

And all that is without mentioning what a great social activity it is. Unless you're dancing on your own, in a hermetically-sealed chamber, then you'll naturally meet many other people both when learning and when putting it out there for real.

So the real (if somewhat clichéd) question is... why wouldn't you?

Why Dance with a Partner?

If you learn partner dancing — where two people dance together in a coordinated manner (beginners may delete the word 'coordinated') — there are yet more benefits. Learn the right partner dance and you are learning a language that transcends borders, allowing you to enjoy the company of someone even if you can't understand a single word they say. To paraphrase a Cuban guy I met whilst researching Dancing Feat, "Dance is not just a set of moves to learn — it's a communication between two people."

Dancing with someone — rather than just at or near them — adds a whole new dimension. You can bond with that person and share a moment together, even if that moment consists largely of lying on the floor trying to disentangle yourselves. If you're single it can give you a great way to meet and interact with other singles. If you're in a relationship it can add a new physicality — a new intimacy, even — to your relationship. And even if you're just out with friends, it gives you an activity which can allow you to bond and have fun with them.

Why Learn on your Travels?

Let's face it, travelling for pleasure is generally pretty good fun no matter how you do it. But travelling with some kind of objective, rather than just for the sake of it, can give you a richer, deeper and more satisfying experience than you might otherwise have. You'll also have a more solid platform from which to boast about your travels when you return home. For more on this idea, see my TEDx talk, Travel with a Narrative (wanderingdesk.com/travel/tedx-travel-narrative/).

Learning to dance whilst on your travels, in a country where dance is part of the culture, is something that offers that deeper experience. Let me go into that in some more detail.

For a start, it's a great way to connect with the country. You can stare at cathedrals and mountains and stuff all you like but, short of chiselling bits off the various sights and eating them, you're always going to feel disconnected from a place if all you're doing is visually inspecting it. To dance with local people to the local rhythms is to truly connect with the place you are in. And if you're learning a dance with a local flavour you can't help but get a deeper sense of the culture of that country.

It's a great way to engage with local people, as it makes great common ground for a conversation. If someone asks you "What are you doing here?" the answer "I'm here to learn how to dance" is always going to generate more interest more than "I'm here to get leathered with other foreigners". Although I suppose it depends who you're talking to. Certainly, whilst I was out there writing Dancing Feat, I found that people were genuinely thrilled by the idea of an outsider unintentionally mangling their proud heritage. And more than just spoken engagement, it gives you a chance to physically interact with locals.

Also, travel is one of the best times to try new things, without people you know judging you, and without your good intentions being stymied by the natural inertia of routine. It's the closest you'll get to suspension of reality — you're surrounded by people who don't know you, and who will likely never see you again. Meaning, with a bit of luck, you'll be buzzing off the simple joy of travel. So the stakes are low, and the excitement is high.

Finally, you'll come back with great stories to tell your friends, beyond just "I went to the place and I saw the thing". The anecdotes will last forever. Admittedly, so will the mental scars, but let's focus on the positives.

Why Learn in Colombia?

Colombia is a great place to learn how to dance, for a whole bunch of reasons:

It has a really strong dance culture

Latin America has a bit of a dance obsession going on, and even by those standards, Colombia still stands out.

There are dance schools everywhere

So you can take classes pretty much anywhere you go. More than that, when you go out at night, the norm is to go dancing. So you'll never have a shortage of opportunities to put what you've learnt into practice.

It's relatively cheap

Whilst there are cheaper countries in the world, Colombia is still a pretty cost-effective place to learn how to dance. It makes hiring a private teacher a realistic option for people who might not be able to afford it in their home country.

Local people will love you

After all you're taking interest in something that Colombians are very proud of, and yet which rarely features in stereotypes about the country. And it's a respectful way of interacting with their country.

It's a great place to go full stop

There are so many things to see and do outside of dancing. Exquisite beaches, jungle-clad ruins, towering peaks, infinite plains, mysterious jungle and many, many other adjective-noun combinations. Check out my book on the subject — 47 Amazing Things to See and Do in Colombia.

Colombia's Dance Culture

So how do people dance in Colombia?

Everywhere

They dance in bars and clubs; at festivals and at parties; inside of venues and out on the street. Okay, so it's not unusual in many parts of the world to go out dancing, but in Colombia it's the main point of the evening. For instance, in my home country of the United Kingdom (should that be 'my home kingdom'?), alcohol is obligatory for a party, whilst dance is optional. In Colombia, the reverse is true. Indeed, you can't even call it a party if there's no dancing.

Together

Almost all dancing in Colombia is done with a partner. There are still clubs where they play rock, pop, techno, *rock-en-espanol* and other genres that support dancing alone, but they aren't the norm.

Naturally

While you can find technically-adept dancing in Colombia, and there are plenty of people who take it seriously (and even pursue it as a career), most people aren't interested in knowing 37 different turns. They just want to feel the *sabor* (flavour), move to the music and have fun.

Is Colombia Safe?

It's a common question, based on a widely-held perception of what Colombia is like.

"For as long as I've known it it's been the place you don't go to. Don't even look at Colombia, people say. Don't even write the word down. If you so much as point to it on a map, men in balaclavas will burst into your room and, at the very least, find a very pointed manner of showing you the difference between gorillas and guerrillas (a particularly annoying ambiguity given they both hang out in jungles)."

Dancing Feat: One Man's Mission to Dance Like a Colombian

So is it safe? Well the real question I suspect you want answering is "Is it safe enough to travel around?" And the answer to that is…

Yes, absolutely.

However, that answer does come with a 'but', so let's go into the situation in more detail.

The headline problems, such as long-term kidnapping, are at levels a fraction of what they were at their peak in 2000. And the country's homicide rate in 2014 was the lowest in decades (although at 12,800 for the year, still not exactly something to boast about).

Street crime, however, is an issue in many towns and cities. We're talking about everything from pickpocketing and bag snatching to knife-point muggings and the spiking of drinks, or even the *paseo millonario*, where a rogue taxi driver and accomplice take you on a forced ATM tour of the city. And despite the recent to-ing and fro-ing in peace negotiations, entire regions of the country are still no-go zones.

What does this mean to you?

It simply means to take care. Check out the current situation using up-to-date sources like the UK's foreign travel advice pages (www.gov.uk/foreign-travel-advice/colombia), or those provided by your own country's government. Travel in numbers. Don't leave your drink unattended, nor accept one from someone you don't know well. Seek local advice on where is safe and not safe to go — it can sometimes vary on a street-by-street basis. Call for taxis — or get your guest house or hotel to do it for you — rather than hailing them on the street. Avoid running with scissors. Don't walk about at night unless you know for sure it's okay.

I meant what I said about the scissors.

Remember that Colombia is not a good country for off-the-beaten-track adventure. I strongly suggest you read the article Some Travelers to Colombia are Plain Stupid (bit.ly/1FzOUt9) by journalist and hostel-owner Richard McColl. And check out this map (www.gov.uk/foreign-travel-advice/colombia) of okay and not-so-okay places issued by the UK FCO. Also keep an eye out for naturally-occurring issues like erupting volcanoes and the like. If you see people running away from one then try and keep up. Yes, I'm being flippant — you can't outrun pyroclastic flow any more than you can surf molten lava. So best just to steer clear.

Of course, I can't tell you about all the possible dangers you might encounter and, besides, things change quickly in the world. It's up to you to do your own research, and to always check with the relevant people, that what you're doing is okay. So if you stab yourself in the eye with a chorizo sausage because the coach hit a bump in the road, then don't come crying to me. Yes, that's a disclaimer.

The most important thing, though, is that you don't let any of this put you off visiting what is an amazing country inhabited by, for the most part, incredibly friendly and giving people.

And finally, just make sure you remember that it's Colombia, not Columbia*, or you'll completely deserve any ills that befall you.

♦

*Just to complicate matters, 'pre-Columbian' is perfectly fine.

[NB: This section first appeared in my book 47 Amazing Things to See and Do in Colombia]

A Quick History Lesson

The history of any country is a complex thing that cannot simply be reduced to a few paragraphs. But what the heck, let's have a go anyway.

Back in the day, the area of land we now call Colombia was populated by lots of different tribes who were just kind of chilling out and making cool-looking stuff out of gold. These were the indigenous people of the Americas, or Amerindians as they're sometimes known. They probably came down from the Caribbean and more northerly parts of the Americas a long time earlier.

Around the year 1498, the Spanish arrived on boats from Europe and proceeded to gallivant through the land, bringing peace and harmony wherever they went (sarcasm alert), and leaving a flower-like scent trail behind them. Assuming that the rotting cadavers of fallen indigenous people smell like flowers, that is.

The Spanish brought with them Catholicism, slaves from Africa and precious foreign diseases, and took away large quantities of gold. As their population increased, racial mixing occurred — after all, it must get kind of lonely if you're a member of a European colonising force that has neglected to include many women. With multiple races now occupying the same lands, the Spanish enforced a kind of racial caste system, generously placing themselves at the top. But as the *criollo* population (those of Spanish ancestry, but born locally) began to increase, so did resentment at the privileges of those born in mainland Spain, as well as the control and influence of Spain in general.

Eventually, people took up arms over this, with the result that Colombia became independent in 1810. And then again in 1819. It was kind of messy like that. Indeed, the blood wasn't all mopped up until about 1823.

Independence might have been won, but political stability

would remain more elusive, with the two main sides —
Liberal and Conservative — bickering constantly, and even
engaging in armed conflict. Things never fully calmed down,
and, in 1949, furore over the murder of a Liberal Party
presidential candidate quickly escalated into long-term
countrywide violence and retribution — a period known as
La Violencia (The Violence).

In the era following this, social inequality spurred the
formation of left-wing guerrilla groups like the FARC
(Revolutionary Armed Forces of Colombia). These were
followed into existence by right-wing paramilitary groups,
which emerged to protect the interests of landowners and
others from said guerrillas. Then, just to really stir things up,
the drugs trade came to prominence. In the 1990s, the main
cartels were broken up, and, from about the year 2000
onwards, the country's crime rate gradually started to come
down. As a direct consequence, the country emerged as a
realistic tourist destination, bringing us to where we are today.

[NB: *This section first appeared in my book 47 Amazing Things to
See and Do in Colombia*]

An Even Quicker Geography Lesson

Colombia has everything. Not content with a coastline on both the Pacific and the Atlantic Oceans, it also has a slice of the Amazon (the world's largest rainforest), three cordilleras of the Andes mountains, two mighty valleys, hugely expansive plains and even a desert. And, with the altitude varying so much, it also has a wide range of eco-systems, with all the associated diversity in flora and fauna (that's plants and animals, for those not acquainted with guidebook parlance).

"It's the place where South America begins; where Central America's dwindling bough suddenly engorges into a full-on trunk; where the great mountainous spine of the Americas explodes into the swashbuckling horde of peaks, plateaus and volcanoes known as the Andes. It's also the place that took on the name of that great explorer Christopher Columbus, the man who would have discovered the Americas had some other people (the Vikings) not discovered them first, and had there not also been a whole bunch of people living there already."

Dancing Feat: One Man's Mission to Dance Like a Colombian

[NB: This section first appeared in my book 47 Amazing Things to See and Do in Colombia]

13

Colombia's Musical Geography

The folk dances of Colombia offer an insight into the rich history and diverse culture of the country. Colombia's ethnic makeup consists mainly of (a) the people that were already there (the Indigenous Peoples), (b) the people who turned up and suddenly decided they owned the place (the Europeans) and (c) the people who were brought there forcibly and made to work (mainly Africans).

The Coasts

Colombia has two coastlines, and it's here where you'll find much of the country's African culture.

The Atlantic (or Caribbean) coast is the land of sunshine and rum, and home to an exuberant music and dance culture. Drumming and percussion play a central role in the traditional music of the region, whilst the dances tend to be more flamboyant than those of the interior, from the frenetic electrical impulses of mapalé to the *¡mirame!* ('Look at me!') of Colombian cumbia. The Pacific coast, meanwhile, is the home to the lulling marimba-based folk genre *currulao*. This latter region, however, is difficult to access, and much of it was unsafe to visit at the time of writing.

Whilst all the favourite Latin genres can be heard on the Caribbean coast, the big three are reggaeton, *vallenato* and *champeta*. There's still salsa here, just less than in other parts, and with perhaps more of a nod to Cuba than to Cali (see further down). Due to the clement weather, informal parties often take place on the streets, sometimes with a speaker stack setup known as a *picó*, although you're unlikely to experience this if you stick to the tourist centres.

Partner dancing in general tends to be done closer in these regions, to the point that it can be surprising for an outsider to see just how sensually two people can dance without there being any romantic connection.

The Mountains

It's a widely held belief on the coast that people from the interior can't dance very well. Certainly, as the altitude increases, the impulse to dance seems to go in the opposite direction. And there's definitely less dancing on the streets as a result of a less-favourable climate. The regional folk dances — often a good indicator of local dance attitudes — are certainly more restrained and conservative, often being tied to a more European culture, such as contradanse. There is also an indigenous Andean dance culture in the south of the country, where Colombia meets Ecuador. This is broadly reflective of the racial mix of the highlands.

But it's all relative of course — there is still a strong dance culture here. And whilst dance can seem less of a priority in some of the smaller, more rural places, people still party like mad things in the bars and clubs of the cities.

The Plains

There are precious few large settlements in this part of the country, as most people live in the mountains and valleys or on the coasts. The plains are home to Llanero (plains) culture, which is very much related to life on the range, as the plains are prime cattle-raising territory. So prepare yourself for checked shirts, cowboy hats and, well, lots and lots of cows. The region has its own musical culture — *música llanera* (the music of the plains) — of which the best known genre is *joropo*. The main instrument is generally the harp, played in devilishly intricate rhythms in 3/4 time, whilst the associated dance is a high-speed mixture of turns and flamenco-like foot stamps.

Cali

The city of Cali deserves a special mention in its own right. Known as 'The Salsa Capital of the World', the city is obsessed with all things salsa. Despite being inland, in one of the country's two major valleys, it has something of a coastal feel, perhaps due in part to its climate.

Which City?

Pretty much every town and city in Colombia has at least one dance school to choose from. Most will be able to school you in the basic urban favourites — salsa, merengue, bachata, reggaeton, *vallenato* — as well as folk dances specific to that region. Cities are often better places to learn simply because the nightlife is generally more active, so you have more opportunity to put it out there and practise. But that aside you can learn pretty much anywhere.

Here are a few of the better-known places.

Bogotá

Set on a plateau in the mountains, Bogotá is the capital, and a city of nearly 9 million inhabitants.

The upsides of learning here are that it's well connected to the rest of the country, and there are plenty of dance opportunities. The downsides are the sheer size of the place — making it time-consuming to navigate — and the climate. Put it this way — if you've come to South America hoping for some sun, you might be disappointed with the average temperature of 58°F (14°C).

Backpackers tend to congregate in the colonial barrio of La Candelaria, though there aren't that many dance opportunities here. For the uptown, upmarket action, head to the north, to the *zona rosa* (the name for the main clubbing district in most towns and cities) and Parque 93.

Medellín

Medellín is Colombia's comeback kid. Has a city ever undergone such a positive transformation in such a short space of time as has Medellín? That's a rhetorical question, and it would take a lot of research to answer fully, so let's just leave it hanging. Regardless, in a short period of time the city has transformed from a dangerous-as-hell place, and one synonymous with drug violence, into the poster-boy of Colombia: all statues, modern buildings and tourists trying to invent new and humorous juxtapositions of themselves with Botero's plump sculptures.

It's known as 'The city of eternal spring' for its year-round temperate climate, but perhaps 'silicone valley' would be a good second nickname — plastic surgery is common here. The climate, and the beauty of the local female populace, means it has a burgeoning international population of English teachers, digital nomads and pick-up artists.

In dance terms, it's a home from home for the Argentine Tango: ever since tango maestro Carlos Gardel died in a plane crash here, the city and the dance have been locked in a passionate clinch. Also popular here is *porro*, a descendant of cumbia, and a genre more normally associated with the coast. But the fact is that you can learn any of the major urban Latin dances here. There are plenty of dance schools, and no shortage of places to go out and practise, from the *zona rosa* in the city's north to the disco enclave of Barrio Colombia.

Cali

All of Colombia likes to dance, but Cali takes it to another level. And for Colombians, Cali means just one thing – salsa.

"Cali isn't just about salsa, Cali is salsa. Cut Cali and it bleeds salsa. Get Cali drunk and it vomits salsa. Inflate Cali and stamp on it and... oh you get the point."

Dancing Feat: One Man's Mission to Dance Like a Colombian

Cali is a hot and sticky place, but not usually oppressively so, and if the temperature gets too hot you can just head up into the Andes to cool off. In attitude, the city definitely associates itself with the coast more than it does with the interior, despite being separated from the Pacific Ocean by a

18

strand of mountains.

Salsa here is danced Cali-style, often known in other parts of the world simply as 'Colombian-style'. It's a very upright style of dancing, with lots of nimble footwork, and sometimes with acrobatics thrown in. They like their salsa fast here, and listen to styles from all over, though plenty of home-grown talent gets played, too, such as Orquesta Guayacán.

Cali is a great place to learn to dance, as there are more dance teachers and schools here than any other city in Colombia. And despite the city's focus on salsa, all the other Latin dance-floor staples are also taught here, plus ballroom and more. There are Pacific influences here, too, such as the marimba-based *currulao*.

The nightlife is great, as you might imagine. But be warned: if you go out to a club with locals, your chances of being able to spend the night sitting down are pretty slim — they'll practically frog-march you to the dance floor. Many clubs in Cali are salsa-only, but there are still plenty of places playing a mixture of Latin styles — something known as *crossover*. The main nightlife areas are Avenida Sexta (the *zona rosa*), plus Menga and Juanchito, both of which are good if you want to carry on dancing when other parts of the city will have stopped by law. There are also little clubs dotted around, one of the best of which is the famous Tin Tin Deo.

The city's main party is the Feria de Cali, held every year in December, when there are parades, parties and even a salsadrome, whilst the Petroneo Alvarez festival is a great opportunity to experience the music from the nearby Pacific coast.

Cartagena

Cartagena was the gateway through which the Spanish performed a lot of their import/export activities, with slaves coming in from Africa, and gold going out the other way. Unsurprisingly given its strategic importance, there was also a whole lot of fighting to control the place. Aside from that, this is a stunning colonial gem of a city, with cannon-lined ramparts, cobbled streets and balconied colonial buildings. It's also got its own fair share of beaches and nearby islands. All this not-so-hidden treasure means it's a good place to hang out for a while and learn to dance.

In terms of musical history, it was the birthplace of legendary *música tropical* singer Joe Arroyo, as well as that of Colombian record label Discos Fuentes.

There aren't many dance school options in the centre, but there are plenty of clubs to go and practise in, both in the colonial centre (and adjoining backpacker area of Getsemaní) and the condo-lined beach front of Boca Granada. *Vallenato*, *champeta* and reggaeton are particularly common in this part of the country. There is also a plethora of Cuban-themed bars, some of them playing live salsa. Plus, if you're lucky, you might see a dance troupe performing the frenetic folk dance of *mapalé* on the streets.

Barranquilla

Many visitors to Colombia bypass Barranquilla in the headlong rush from Cartagena to Santa Marta. But that's exactly why you should go to Barranquilla. It might not have quite the same colonial charm as its two neighbours, but it's a great place to come if you want an authentic Colombian experience, and to spend your time with a greater proportion of local people as opposed to tourists.

Barranquilla is known for having a vibrant nightlife and there are plenty of places to go out in this part of town. Expect to hear a lot of *vallenato*, *champeta* and reggaeton here, along with a smattering of salsa, as per much of the coast. There's also a really good museum — the Museo del Caribe (Museum of the Caribbean) — which gives a great insight into the local coastal culture, including the music and dance (though note that on my last visit it was entirely in Spanish).

To the rest of Colombia, Barranquilla is synonymous with carnival. The Barranquilla Carnival is reputedly the second largest parade festival in the world after that at Rio de Janeiro, and culminates in several days of parades and festivities in which you can experience the best of Colombian party culture

Pasto

Isolated in the far south of the country, Pasto is usually the last stopping point for people heading south to Ecuador, or the first for those arriving from there. It's located in the Andes, at the foot of the Galeras volcano, with its frequent digestive rumblings. Perhaps it's been eating too much of the local speciality — *cuy* (guinea pig). Pastuzos (the people of Pasto) are the butt of many a Colombian joke, but in reality they're pretty quick with the wisecracks themselves, and are some of the friendliest people in a very friendly country.

There are a couple of notable dance schools here, and it's a decent, friendly place to learn one of the Latin staples, or even a regional Andean number like guaneña. Note that at 2,500m above sea-level, it's not only a mite chilly, but that dancing here is a good way of feeling like a 20-a-day smoker with asthma. Pasto has its own small strip of regular discos, but for a proper Andean night out you should head to a *peña* — an Andean music venue where a live band plays a mixture of Latin staples, along with local Andean favourites.

Villavicencio

Villavicencio is a place that most tourists don't go anywhere near, and is also the largest city in a sparsely populated part of the country. It's the gateway to the country's Llanos (Plains) — a vast, flat cattle-farming region which extends into neighbouring Venezuela in the north, and eventually coalesces into the Amazon Basin in the east. A taxi-ride from the centre up to the viewpoint at restaurant La Piedra del Amor will give you a feel for how the Andes suddenly give up being all high and pointy and come crashing down into nothingness.

There are a number of dance schools here teaching urban dances, though if you really want a challenge, have a go at the local foot-stamping favourite of *joropo*. In terms of nightclubs, the usual Latin favourites can be found in the *zona rosa*, but there are also a couple of folk music places where you can also have a go at spanking the floor like a local: El Botalón and Pentagrama Llano y Folclor.

Others

Pick a city, any city and the chances are you'll be able to find a dance school or individual teaching whatever it is that interests you, plus a whole bunch of nightclubs in which to practise it. There are plenty of places beyond the ones I've mentioned here: Bucaramanga; Ibague; one of the three coffee zone cities of Armenia, Pereira and Manizales, all of which are in the mountains; Neiva, in the upper reaches of the Magdalena Valley; Valledupar — the spiritual home of the *vallenato* genre; or any number of smaller places.

Check Internet sources to make sure that wherever you're going is safe, and then strike out, get lessons and have some fun.

Which Dance?

Most people who come to Latin America thinking 'I want to learn to dance' have probably already mentally appended 'salsa' to the end of the sentence, such is the prevalence of that genre, and its strong association with this part of the world. But it doesn't hurt to know what your options are, and besides, there's a dance which I think is much better for beginners to learn than salsa. I'll come to that in the next section.

Broadly speaking, you can group the dance and music into two main types: urban and folkloric (folk).

When I talk about urban dances, I'm referring to the types they dance in nightclubs. They're not necessarily part of Colombian heritage — they're more of a general Latin thing with roots in places like Cuba, the Dominican Republic and so on — but they tend to be danced all over Colombia, if not Latin America. In general, we're talking about formalised partner dances like salsa, bachata, merengue and *vallenato*, plus the more freeform reggaeton.

Folkloric dances meanwhile tend to be more deeply rooted in Colombia's cultural heritage, and are generally region-specific. You might occasionally see them danced in nightclubs, but generally only in the area in which they're from.

How do I choose a dance?

To choose a dance, you need to think about what your motivations are for learning to dance in the first place.

Do you want to learn something which will enable you to dance in nightclubs and at parties all over Colombia? Something which you'll also be able to use in other parts of the world, and which will provide a solid basis for future social dance learning? If so, then you should learn an urban dance.

Do you want a unique and authentic cultural experience? Something which will impress locals and give you a flavour of what it means to be from that particular part of Colombia, but which you won't be able to use back home (and will even be of limited use in Colombia itself)? Then learn a folkloric dance.

Be Realistic

All dances are harder than they look, so if a dance looks very hard, it almost certainly is (and then some). Weigh up how much time and money you can genuinely afford to invest in this. If you can only manage an hour a day for five days, then you'll struggle to scratch the surface of something like *mapalé*. I'll go into the specifics of how long it will likely take to learn each dance in the next section.

Pick a genre you like

It's going to sound really obvious, but it's really important that you actually like the dance that you're learning. Otherwise, what is your motivation to get any good at it? You're going to need to practise outside your dance classes and that generally requires you to give a damn. So search it out on Youtube in advance — even the most obscure folk genre has been recorded and uploaded by somebody, somewhere. And seek it out live on location to see what it's like in the flesh. Ask yourself how you feel about the tone of the dance (intimate, joyous, frenzied)? About the music? About the proximity of the dancers? Can you see yourself doing this dance?

That said, remember that how a dance looks and how it feels can be very different. Merengue, for instance, can look a bit silly on first impressions due to its hip-swinging nature. But it's tremendous fun to do, and also a relatively easy dance to pick up, so it's best not to judge purely on aesthetics.

Or maybe pick all of them

If you have the time and inclination, consider taking dance classes in multiple genres. This is more ambitious and requires either (a) much more time or (b) acceptance that you'll likely be no better than mediocre in any of them. But learn all the urban favourites, for instance, and you'll be able to stay on the dance floor all night without having to worry about what's coming up, because you'll know how to dance to it. This was one of my aims in Dancing Feat, and if you can achieve it, it will put you in a great situation.

Dance Class Specifics

Let's look at those dances, and the associated music, in some more detail.

Salsa

Globally, salsa is the big one. It has its origins in Cuba and New York, with a dash of Puerto Rico, but its worldwide popularity means there's been an explosion of styles and variations. It shouldn't come as a surprise, therefore, that Colombia has its very own version of the dance.

Cali-style salsa (aka salsa Caleña or Colombian-style salsa) is a fast, upright style with fancy flourishes of the feet. This makes it great exercise for both body and mind, and means when you get home you can show off your footwork to your friends without the minor inconvenience of having to carry a dance partner with you everywhere you go.

Already know another style of salsa (e.g. New York or LA)? Unfortunately, this will be about as useful in Colombia as Welsh. Well, okay, I'm exaggerating a little — having learnt some salsa will definitely stand you in good stead — but other forms of salsa fit with Cali-style about as well as Lego blocks do with Stickle Bricks. But if Cali-style salsa is so specific, is it worth learning?

Absolutely. For a start, it does get danced in other parts of the world, even if it's not as popular as Cuban, LA or NY-style. Secondly, it's a great way of getting used to the rhythms of the salsa music itself, which can take a little time for some. Thirdly, some of the steps, like the mambo (read: going forwards and backwards), are common to most types of salsa. And finally, it means you get to have a great time in Cali, not to mention nightclubs in the rest of Colombia.

As you might imagine, if you want to learn Cali-style salsa, the best place to go is Cali. Indeed, there are more dances schools in Cali than anywhere else in Colombia. But it's such a universal genre that you'll find it taught almost everywhere.

To have a decent grasp of the basics you'll need a minimum of 10 hours of tuition. You should double that if you want to learn a few flashy turns. Beyond that you can just keep going. People spend years getting good at salsa, so don't expect to master it in a single intensive period.

Merengue

Merengue is the national dance and music of the Dominican Republic, but is danced all over Latin America. It can look faintly comical to a foreigner — the sight of two people swinging their hips in unison is hard to take seriously — but give it a go and you'll find it's tremendous fun and, in my opinion, the single best entry point into Latin dance.

Indeed, if you're short of time and only plan to learn one dance my recommendation would be to learn merengue. It's much quicker to learn than salsa, and is danced just about everywhere. And the fact that it's danced to such a simple two-step rhythm means that if you mess up, you don't have to wait around a whole bar for the beat, as with salsa or bachata, so it's much more forgiving and hence ideal for beginners. With the leg movements being so simple by comparison with other dances, you can focus on learning the mechanics of the turns that are common to so many partner dances (such as salsa and bachata). It's also a great primer in many of the other basic dance skills, such as how to shift your weight, leading and following and how to apologise to a complete stranger for any dance injuries you may have inflicted.

Finally, it's omnipresent in Latin American, and you should find it taught at most schools in Colombia.

I'll say it again — if you're going to learn one dance, learn merengue.

Vallenato

Vallenato is an odd one. You'll see the CDs being sold

from supermarkets and street stalls alike featuring oiled-up bikini-clad women. Then you'll hear the music featuring an accordion and cheesy lyrics and you'll wonder if the people who designed the covers ever actually listened to it. It's also slightly peculiar in that it's a very folkloric-sounding style of music that is played in urban environments. Despite all this, *vallenato* is much cherished in Colombia, and the genre with the best claim to being the national music of Colombia.

Vallenato is etched in the Colombian psyche like a love heart carved in the trunk of a tree. It's what couples dance to when they want to get close to each other, and what groups of men listen to when they want to get close to some alcohol. You'll hear it all over the country, and it towers over everything else once you get anywhere near the Caribbean coast. That said, in some parts of the country it gets less love, and in somewhere like Cali, a *vallenato* number can pretty much clear a dance floor.

The dance form is about as basic as partner dancing gets. But that doesn't mean it doesn't have some steps to it, and complicating the matter is the fact that the music comes in four different rhythms. The footwork is simple, and the turns are even simpler, so it can be learned quite quickly. The slowest, most intimate style doesn't even require feet movements: you just hold each other very close and roll your hips in unison to fill the four beats.

It's not a particularly exhilarating exciting dance, but the ubiquity of the music makes it a useful one to learn. The main obstacle for foreigners is a dislike of the music — it all tends to sound the same at first — but I can vouch from experience that it really can grow on you, too, especially if you know how to dance to it.

You could probably learn everything you need to know about the dance in two to five hours of personal tuition. To experience it, you're best heading to the Caribbean coast, ideally to Valledupar, its spiritual home. It's simple enough that it's one of the few dances that you could potentially nail just from watching others, but you'll still cut out all that awkward uncertainty by going for classes.

Bachata

Bachata is originally from the Dominican Republic, but doesn't seem have a natural home in Colombia in the way of the other Latin staples. However, most clubs will play some from time to time (if less frequently than, say, salsa, merengue and reggaeton), and it has gained a global popularity, so it can be a useful dance to learn. Note that the style danced in Colombia is fairly rudimentary in comparison to some other parts of the world.

The signature move of bachata is the tap of the foot (and elegant roll of the hip) on the last beat of the bar. Trickily, the same foot then moves again straight away, requiring a counter-intuitive weight shift. Combine this with the fact that it's danced quite closely — often with legs interleaved — and the result is a fair amount of toe-treading amongst beginners. So it's probably best learned in shoes with closed toes, or at least ones that are black and blue to help camouflage any bruising.

You can certainly learn bachata in Colombia, although you might find that it's not in the same super-intimate style as often seen in Europe. It would still be a good start, though. As with salsa, reckon on about 10 hours to do the basics to a passable standard, and 20 or more to start making real progress.

Reggaeton

Reggaeton is the bad boy of the Latin music scene. It's the one with all the hard beats and the attitude, and also the one most likely to feature a non-ironic 'I'm on a boat' style video, replete with scantily-clad women, designer sunglasses and immaculately stencilled facial hair. Born in Panama and refined in Puerto Rico, it's a fusion of dancehall, soca, hip hop and other genres all layered over the trademark Dem Bow riddim (the *thump-de thump-derr* of kick drum and snare).

The style of dancing most normally associated with reggaeton is *perreo* — the archetypal 'sex with clothes on'. Translating as 'doggy-style' (ahem), *perreo* is a bump-and-grind style of couple dancing, with a whole lot of the woman bending over and pressing her backside against, else in the general direction of, the man's groin. Dancing opposite each other often includes the interlocking of legs, the man raising one of the woman's legs by the thigh, and generally suggestive pelvic movements.

It is possible to dance with a similar attitude but with less intimacy. Some people will forego the most intimate clinches, and in some parts of the country friends will often form a circle to dance to reggaeton, taking it in turns to go (or be dragged into) the centre to show off fly moves.

Attitudes to reggaeton vary. Some find the lyrics misogynistic and the *perreo* style of dancing too intimate. Certainly, *perreo* tends to be more accepted on the coast, where dancing in general tends to be closer and more sensual. Indeed, many locals believe that this level of intimacy in a dance means nothing. Certainly, many a foreigner has come unstuck thinking that there's been more between them and someone they've been dancing with than has actually existed.

The good thing about reggaeton is that there are no fixed steps to be executed in time with the music. But it's still worthwhile taking classes, as there can be few sights more tragic than that of someone trying but failing to be sexy, or to have attitude. It's also a really good one to complement existing skills in something like salsa, as it requires the movements of very different body parts and requires a very different attitude. You might want to have a think about what level of closeness you're comfortable with in advance, though.

Folk

There are many different types of folk dance in Colombia — certainly far too many to cover here. For Dancing Feat, I learnt four different folk styles and had a lot of fun doing it.

The thing to note is that, for the most part, your opportunities to dance these styles in a night club scenario will be limited, and will be practically zero once you've left the country. In other words, this is something you would do just for the hell of it, though you'll undoubtedly have some fun, bond with locals and get to experience something a bit different.

If you're on the Caribbean coast, *mapalé* is an amazing dance — frenetic with erotic undertones (they were problem overtones at one time, but things move on). However, it's as difficult as they come, and would take a serious investment of time to get good. It's also a lot of hard work in the coastal heat.

Cumbia might be a better choice in this region, as you can learn the basics to a passable level in about 5 hours, and it does sometimes get played in clubs and other social events. It would certainly be useful during Carnival in Barranquilla, as I found when I took my seat in a stand next to the parade.

"As I sit there, enjoying my new, lofty position, a bright yellow t-shirt with a young woman inside approaches me, and pulls me to my feet. Okay, so what's all this about?

It clicks.

No! No! No! Wait! You don't understand! I'm not here to dance — I'm just a spectator! Look, I had specific assurances! Dammit why didn't I go for the most boring looking stand?

I'm still working out the least impolite way of making it clear that no dancing is about to occur, when I'm spotted by everyone in a fifty metre radius. Whoops go up all round the palco (stand), and I know that, in dance terms at least, I've passed the point of no return. Mind you, I probably passed that point the moment I boarded a plane for

Colombia."

Dancing Feat: One Man's Mission to Dance Like a Colombian

Note that this style of cumbia, as danced on Colombia's Caribbean coast, is nothing like the one danced in other parts of Latin America. The Colombian one involves a shuffling gait with which the man approaches and tries to woo his female dance partner using his *sombrero vueltiao* (the iconic hat of the coast), whilst the woman ruffles her skirt and attempts to balance a bottle of rum on her head.

Joropo, with its flamenco and waltz-like elements would be the obvious choice for the plains. It's also a cross-border genre, being the national dance of Venezuela. *Joropo* is an amazing dance to watch and it's not just for show — people dance it for real in dedicated clubs. The main issue is that it's a complicated dance with numerous different elements to master and would take maybe 10-20 hours just to get the basics down, and many more to reach the level where you're striking sparks off the floor.

If you want to learn an Andean dance, then try one of the mountainous departments such as Boyacá or Santander, north of Bogotá, where they have dances such as the gentle *torbellino*. You could also consider heading to Pasto in the southern Andes. Here you can learn the springy *guaneña* or *sanjuanito* styles, to the sound of panpipes, with a half-decent chance of dancing them in a *peña* (live music club in the Andes).

If you are going to a festival which is related to a specific dance, then it can be a good idea to learn that particular dance, as you will definitely feel more a part of what's going on. For instance, it could be fun to learn some basic *currulao* for the Pacific Music Festival (aka Petronio Álvarez) in Cali, for instance. You'll certainly impress the heck out of the locals with your quick-stepping and *pañuelo*-waving.

How to Recognise the Music

Music and dance in Latin America are for the most part inextricably linked. Each musical genre has a particular way of dancing to it, and this makes sense — you wouldn't dance the hokey cokey to the tune of the can can. Although maybe that's a pity. Anyway, for this reason, it's really helpful to be able to recognise the various genres of music they play in a typical Colombian nightclub. Learning to dance is challenging — you probably don't want to complicate the matter by trying to map bachata moves to a merengue rhythm.

If you're in a salsa-only nightclub then you won't have any problems — asking what genre is playing would be like going into a pound shop and asking how much each item costs. But a lot of Colombian nightclubs don't play a single genre and instead play a bit of everything. It's quite common to have 15 minutes of merengue, 15 minutes of salsa and so on. And if you don't know what's what, then how will you know when to get up and dance? Just to confuse matters, or maybe just to confuse foreigners, some artists record songs that cross genres, mixing salsa with reggaeton for example.

This is not a problem for locals. Obviously, they can identify most genres of music. But also, they can also recognise many tracks purely from the intro, without having to wait for some kind of genre-identifying beat. Finally, they can dance passably to most if not every genre of music that's likely to play, so even if they don't recognise the track at first — or even at all — it doesn't matter, because they'll be able to dance to it.

But what about you? Well, you could just learn to identify your own genre — e.g. salsa — and that would certainly help. But it's actually best learning all of the most common ones, for a number of reasons. The more genres you can identify, the quicker you'll be able to rule other genres out. After all, if you're learning bachata, then it helps to be able to rule out what isn't bachata. Plus it's empowering and fun as a visitor to the country to be able to name everything that's playing. It also means you'll feel more a part of what's going on, and feel more comfortable in the club environment in general. In short, you'll have a greater sense of control over your situation, which is good news if the thought of flaunting your amateur moves in public makes you feel nervous. Spending time in nightclubs will mean this happens automatically, but deliberately and systematically learning the genres can get you to this stage much more quickly than by osmosis.

Which genres do you need to be able to recognise? Well, I'd suggest the five main urban genres from the previous section, namely salsa, merengue, *vallenato*, bachata and reggaeton. Other genres do crop up from time to time — I've heard cha-cha-cha, reggae, *música llanera*, *mapalé*, cumbia, *currulao* and all sorts of other things in Colombian nightclubs — but getting those five urban ones will give you a good ratio of reward for time invested.

So how do you go about this? Well I'd recommend you go to Youtube or Spotify and search for playlists for salsa, merengue, bachata, reggaeton and vallenato. Just do a search on those terms and you'll find something. Put it on in the background and let it wash over you, and you'll soon get a feel for it. Nail it further still by doing some deep listening. In other words, sit there focusing on the music and ask yourself "What instruments are playing? What are the most noticeable rhythms? What is the one thing that seems to typify this genre?"

For example, almost all reggaeton has the distinctive *thump-der thump-derrr* beat in it at some point, otherwise known as the Dem Bow riddim. It's unmistakable. And merengue has a *chikka-chum chikka-chum* rice shaker sound. There's far more to it than that, but having an entry point can really help. With time you'll stop having to think about it — you'll just know what it is you're listening to.

Also useful can be listening to local Colombian radio via internet websites / apps like tunein (tunein.com/search/?query=colombia). This will help you become familiar with the specific songs you're likely to hear — both the classics and current hits — to the point where you'll recognise them just from the intro. So instead of having to wait for the giveaway rhythm to begin, you'll hear the opening chords and say "Oh - it's Fruko y Sus Tesos!" and look for a partner to dance some salsa with. Just like the locals do.

As a side note, whilst writing this section I've discovered that listening to merengue increases my typing speed.

Finding Schools

Finding dance schools and/or dance teachers is much like finding any other service in a city. The Internet is a pretty good source, as you might imagine, although not everyone has a presence there, so it's worth considering other possibilities. I'll list both. As a side note, you may need to use the translate feature of your browser, or Google Translate (translate.google.com) if your Spanish isn't up to scratch, as many sites won't be in English.

First some Internet sources:

Páginas Amarillas

Páginas Amarillas (www.paginasamarillas.com.co), or 'Yellow Pages', is a trade directory for all Latin America, with sub-sites for the various countries. It's the single best starting point for finding schools. Type 'Escuelas De Baile' (Dance Schools) and the name of the town or city into the relevant boxes and hit search and you'll get as comprehensive a list as you can find anywhere.

Google

Consider using the Colombian version (www.google.com.co) to get results that are more geographically relevant. This is especially useful if you're searching on Cali, as the results page will otherwise favour 'California' (you can also add 'Colombia' to your search terms to help with this). Remember that many pages will be in Spanish, although if your Spanish isn't great then consider searching in English anyway, as schools with English-language sections are suggestive of them offering classes in English and/or being accustomed to teaching foreigners in general.

Google maps

Zoom into the city of your choice and type 'baile', 'danza'

or 'dance' in to the search box. This is particularly useful for finding a dance school close to your accommodation. Here is a search on 'danza' in Bucaramanga: goo.gl/maps/RSuww.

Facebook
Type in 'baile', 'danza' or 'dance' or the name of the specific dance (e.g. salsa) plus the city name into the search bar to get a list of groups and pages either for dance in general or specific dance schools. For example, there's a page about salsa schools in Cali (www.facebook.com/escuelasdesalsa).

Couchsurfing
Couchsurfing is a global social network allowing visitors to connect with local people and possibly stay with them. There aren't generally listings here, but you can connect with locals and ask about recommended dance schools, either individually or by going to one of the discussion groups, like this one for Barranquilla (www.couchsurfing.com/groups/cs-barranquilla).

Now some more-traditional sources:

Tourist Offices
In my own experience, tourist offices rarely have much information about dance schools, but they can be worth a go. During my own journey, the one in Cali was the only one to have a pre-made list of schools.

Hostels
Ask at a hostel reception, even if you're not staying in one, and also check their noticeboard. It's a fairly common request in backpacker-friendly places, so there's a good chance they'll know places, and may even have an agreement with a dance teacher to come along and teach in situ. Again, this is a good

way of finding an English-language dance lesson.

Convenience stores

As odd as it might sound, asking in the small convenience stores you find on street corners all over Colombia is a good idea, as these places often act as the hub of the community. Expect to have to speak Spanish.

Choosing a School

There are lots of factors which go into choosing a dance school. Here are a few things you might want to factor in:

Location

If it takes you half an hour to get to your dance school, and another half an hour to get back, and you do this twice a day, then you're losing two hours a day just in commuting. If you want to learn how to commute then this is a good idea, otherwise it's a lot of time wasted and could be quite a sap on your motivation levels.

Then there's the issue of safety. Is the *barrio* (neighbourhood) okay? Will you have to go through somewhere dodgy en route to get there? Can you get there by public transport, or are you going to be reliant on taxis? In which case, have you factored that into the cost of the lessons?

Teacher

The teacher is the single most important part of the equation. Some schools are a one-man (or woman) band, whereas others will have a number of teachers available. Normally the school will assign you a teacher based on your needs, rather than you doing the choosing. This isn't a brothel, after all. Actually, I have no idea how brothels work.

It might be an idea to have a taster lesson with a teacher before booking a whole series just to be sure it's going to work out. That way you can find the answers to some important questions. Do they seem to be proficient in the dance you want to learn? Is there a language barrier? And do you actually get on?

If you're having one-to-one lessons in a partner dance, having a teacher of the opposite sex will usually make the most sense, as it means you can partner up with your dance teacher (society dictates that partner dances are almost invariably one man with one woman). However, the person who best knows what you yourself should be doing is a teacher of the same sex as you (the roles are not identical — see leading and following). One solution would be to have two teachers, so you can cover both roles. This is probably overkill if you're learning on your own, it will likely double the cost and also can be a bit annoying as you'll have two separate people fussing over you and correcting your mistakes. Still, it could work quite well if you're in a couple.

Facilities

As long as the basics are in place – a floor to dance on and a mirror to preen in – the physical space is unlikely to cause problems, but you should still go and check it out before committing as this is where you'll be spending most of your time. It can also give important clues as to how well run the school is. Do bear in mind, though, that all dance schools tend to be a little beat-up — it's a sign of the hard graft that goes on there — so don't have expectations of it looking like a health spa.

One thing worth enquiring about is whether you will have to share the dance floor (and sound system) with students doing completely different classes at the same time, as this can be quite disruptive. Also, if you're in a hot part of the country, it can be worth checking whether or not the space is air-conditioned.

Graduation

Are you expected to put on a graduation show (*clausura*) at the end? This is where you have to dance in front of the other students, and possibly others. It's not a common setup, but nor is it unknown. Most potential students will be fine with this, but then most students aren't complete dance cowards. Unlike me. I actually think *clausuras* are a great idea as they give you something definitive to aim for, and provide a great memory. They can be kind of stressful, but you'll certainly find yourself practising. Or absconding. One of the two.

"'I've got it!

If I sign up for more lessons, then I won't have to do the clausura! You can't graduate if you're still studying – how much sense would that make? I'll be able to put it off until the next opportunity, which could be easily be another two weeks away. And, hey, maybe I'll just neglect to mention that I'll be gone by then.

'What a shame,' I'll say. 'I'm sooooooo sorry. I've got to catch a bus to the other side of the country!' Then leave, sniggering like a naughty – yet clearly brilliant – schoolboy.

I send Marta an email to this effect. Excluding the 'dastardly plan' elements, obviously – experience has taught me that this reduces the chance of success.

Her response is an agreed set of dates for my new lessons. And an email not to forget the clausura, which still stands. Forget dance footwear: running shoes would have made a better investment. Also, I think I need to read the Art of War."

Dancing Feat: One Man's Mission to Dance Like a Colombian

Dance Classes in Detail

Once you've decided on a school, there are still plenty more choices to navigate.

Private or group classes?

Private lessons are great for people who are limited for time. They also make a lot of sense if you feel self-conscious about your dance abilities, as they mean you can make a mess of things in greater privacy. You also get individual attention, so your mistakes are more likely to get picked up on.

But groups have their own place, too. They're a fraction of the price of private lessons, are a great way of getting practice with lots of different partners and are also useful for meeting other learners, and hence potential practice partners. Since they often teach a variety of different styles in a single lesson, they can also be an excellent introduction to Latin American dancing in general. Don't have any fear of going to a dance group if you don't know what you're doing: there will be plenty of rubbish dancers there — that's why people go to dance school. It should be noted that I say this from a position of total hypocrisy.

I'd argue that the best idea is to go for both: take individual classes by day to gain confidence, and mix it up with locals in group classes by night.

How long, and how frequently, should your classes be?

If you're going to group classes, then you're pretty much at the whim of the school. If you're arranging private lessons, however, you can usually negotiate a mutually-agreeable schedule.

Classes are typically between one or two hours in length or sometimes an hour and a half, with a warm up of 5-15 minutes. Personally, I found my concentration would run dry just before an hour was up, so a two hour lesson needed a break in the middle. I also found one-and-a-half hours to be exactly the wrong time — if I took a break when I needed one then the second part of the lesson was very short. If I split the lesson into equal parts, then the first part felt short given that you also need time to warm up.

My own preference was to take two classes of an hour a day. I found it better than a single class of two hours as your brain has more time to recover, it feels like less of a slog (so less of a strain on your motivation), and you're not paying for the break (although you will need two warm-ups). A good idea might be a class in the morning and another in late afternoon, leaving all day to explore the city and do other things. However, you also have double the travel time to and from the class, so this option is only realistic if the school is near your accommodation.

Isn't it complicated?

If you do take a two hour class then make sure you insist on a break in the middle. In my experience, many teachers will be quite happy to plough on through, perhaps because it's not as mentally taxing for them as it will be for you.

Multiple teachers

If you approach a school at short notice, there's a good chance they won't be able to fulfil your request with one teacher. Do whatever you can to avoid having different teachers from one class to the next. There is no single perfect way of doing any dance, and the last thing you need as a beginner is to have a bunch of different people playing tug-of-war with your style. It's better to be flexible with your time, or even seek out a different school, than to keep changing teachers.

"NO!!!!!!!!!!!!!!!!!!
I've got the legwork wrong? Seriously, you must be having me on.

It's my third lesson, my third teacher, and, now, my third time spending an entire lesson on the basics."

Dancing Feat: One Man's Mission to Dance Like a Colombian

Mind Management

During my time in Colombia, I attempted to learn something like nine or ten different dances, so I became very familiar with the process of learning to dance. One of the main things I learned was that the internal gauge of your own abilities can give you all sorts of false readings. If you're anything like, me you'll experience something like the following:

Stage 1 — Hooray! You're amazing!

After the first lesson or two you'll be buzzing and thinking you've nailed it. You're almost certainly wrong — you're experiencing a false confidence in your own abilities. This is likely for a variety of reasons, but is probably in part because you're not yet skilled enough to recognise your own lack of skill, something known as the Dunning-Kruger effect.

Stage 2 — Gahhh! It's a disaster!

Next comes a massive slump back to earth, when you feel like you know nothing. This isn't true either, of course — you might not be an expert, but you're still more experienced than before you started. Yet strangely you might feel like your dancing is now worse, wondering (with almost comical levels of melodrama) where it all went so wrong since those halcyon days of the first lesson. What's probably happening here is that, as your ability and understanding of the dance increases and your body gains familiarity with the new movements, you're getting a truer sense of your skill level. But this is a lot less then you thought it was, so feels like a big slump.

Stage 3 — Okay! Everything's fine and getting gradually better

After all that early brain noise, you'll be on a more realistic slope. You'll still get off days, of course, but if you keep taking classes and keep practising then overall you'll keep improving. Think of it as one of those share indexes with ups and downs but a generally positive trend.

The key thing to remember from all this is that your brain is an utter swine that likes nothing better than to mess with you. Put simply, you can't trust it, or at least not in those early days. Any sense of elation or despair should be treated with suspicion. Plot an unswerving course through the nonsense by continuing to learn and to practise regardless and you'll be just fine.

Leading and Following

Most partner dancing follows a simply premise: if there are two of you in the dance, then one person is going to be making the decisions. Otherwise it would be like a car with two steering wheels (or worse, no steering wheels). The person who is making the decisions for the pair is said to be leading. The other person, who responds to their cues, is said to be following.

Leading is tricky. Not only do you have to do your own thing, you also need to guide your partner, so you're effectively thinking for two people. On top of that, you have to be able to communicate your intentions clearly, ideally without yanking any limbs out of their sockets. But following is by no means a breeze, either — you have to remain alert and receptive to the signals of the person leading, and to stay light enough on your feet to be able to respond to their whim.

So how do you know who leads and who follows? With gender roles being so strong in Colombia, a couple almost invariably consists of a man and a woman, with the man leading and the woman following. There are probably all sorts of interesting conversations to be had about this in the area of sexuality and gender politics, but they're outside the scope of this book.

There are various times when you'll encounter exceptions to the one-man-leading-one-woman situation: when dancing reggaeton *perreo*-style (when it could sometimes be said that the woman leads); when dancing certain folk dances (there is at least one where the woman leads); when dancing reggaeton in groups (where no-one is leading); when there are too few men (when some men may dance with two women); and in teaching situations.

Often, one of the two people dancing in your pair will be considerably more skilled than the other, which generally means you'll be limited to the lower of the two abilities.

If you're the one following, and the lead is solid but boring, then it's easy enough to see the dance out. But if they really don't have a clue, then this might leave you in a bit of a quandary. As one Colombian woman told me of a beginner, "He's doing all the right moves … he's just not doing them in time with the music."

I asked Vanessa what she would do if the guy was dancing out of time or badly.

"I think I would just try to keep my pace and let him continue dancing badly, hehehe, until the end of the song. Then I would just run away! Or, I would try to teach him (only if it was someone that I trust completely). My friend has her own strategy (that I could use in the future in Colombia): she just says, 'oops, time to get a beer'"

If you're leading, and you're aware that you're restricting your partner with your limited moves then don't keep asking for repeat dances unless they're happy with that. Conversely, if you're leading and your partner knows fewer moves than you, don't force your partner through long sequences of complicated turns if they're clearly not into it. In Colombia, the idea of dancing is to share the experience of the dance with another person and to have fun, as opposed to showing the rest of the club how freaking amazing you are.

The Language Barrier

Colombia hasn't been on the international tourist / backpacker trail for all that long, so English isn't as widespread as many other places in Central and South America. For that reason, whether you're a prospective dance student or a visitor in general, it can really help if you can speak some Spanish, the official language of Colombia. In dance terms, speaking Spanish means that pretty much every dance teacher in the country is available to you, whereas if you don't then you're limiting yourself to the subset that speak English.

Even so, unless you're fluent, it can still help if your teacher speaks some English (or whatever your native tongue is). Learning a dance can be brain-melting enough without having to contend with a foreign language at the same time. This mostly applies to one-on-one dance classes, where you're likely to be in conversation with your teacher. Group classes tend to have a different dynamic in which it's less important. Indeed, I've attended plenty of group classes where I didn't speak the same language as the instructor, and for the most part it didn't matter, as all the most important stuff was demonstrated physically. I wouldn't necessarily recommend it to a total dance newbie, though — you'll be far enough out of your comfort zone as it is.

Here are a few of the dance-specific Spanish words that you'll come across in Colombia:

	bailar	to dance (*vamos a bailar* — let's dance)
(un)	*baile*	a dance
	brincar	to jump (*no te brinques* — don't jump)
	conducir	to lead (*el hombre suele conducir* — the man usually leads)

	coquetear	to flirt
(una)	*danza*	a dance
	deslizar	to slide
(una)	*figura*	a dance figure
	girar	to turn
	juntito	dancing with your bodies pressed together (see also *pegado*)
(una)	*mano*	a hand (*sube la mano* — raise your hand)
(la)	*música*	the music (*con la música* — with the music)
(un)	*paso*	a step / a unit of footwork
(una)	*patada*	a kick
	pegado	dancing with your bodies pressed together (see also *juntito*)
(un)	*pie*	a foot
(el)	*ritmo*	the rhythm
	subir	to raise (*sube la mano* – raise your hand)
(una)	*vuelta*	a turn
(un)	*zapateo*	a unit of tap-dancing or foot-stamping

For more terms surrounding Colombian music and dance, the Wikipedia glossary of Colombian music is a good resource (en.wikipedia.org/wiki/Glossary_of_Colombian_music).

Proximity and Boundaries

We all carry with us our own ideas — informed by our culture, values and individual life experiences — of what is and isn't appropriate in terms of bodily contact and proximity. And when we travel, these ideas often come into conflict with those of others. There can be few instances where this so obvious as when queuing. Sorry — dancing. Just the Englishman in me.

Navigating this maze of dance-floor appropriateness can be a difficult and awkward experience. You want to be part of what's going on, and to fit in with social mores, but this is difficult because you've got the boundaries of both yourself and others to consider and you don't really know what the rules are in the first place. Where can you put your hands? How close is too close? If someone takes off all their clothes and points to the bed, are they flirting with you?

Just how close you get to your partner depends on a lot of things, such as which part of the country you're in, what genre you're dancing to, how well you know your partner, the preferences or even mood of the individual and, of course, whether or not you're in a cupboard. From a purely geographical side, altitude is a good predictor of proximity — people tend to dance closer together on the coast, and further apart in the mountains.

The furthest-apart hold for partner dances, or at least those where contact occurs, is simply to hold hands. The closest is to have your bodies literally pressed against each other. The middle ground is for the man to have his right hand on the woman's back. The closer you are, the less freedom of movement you have, and so the smaller the steps. In the tightest clinches, you don't even move your feet — you merely gyrate hips together.

So how do you gauge what's appropriate where you are?

Watch how the locals dance

If it's possible, try and take on the role of chin-stroking social anthropologist before you get up and dance. You can definitely get a good feel for what's okay and what's not simply by watching and asking. Also note how people behave after they dance so you can understand the context — is this a couple or are they just friends?

'Mira,' says Oscar, bringing me back to the world of the open-eyed. Look.

Over the road, two people are dancing together. They're stood facing each other, feet opposing feet, but from their knees upwards they're a single indivisible unit, hips gently gyrating in unison.

Okay, so we're watching a couple of lovers dancing together intimately. What are you expecting from me, Oscar. A dig in the ribs and some 'Phwoar — eh!' type comments? I mean, it feels like a minor invasion of their privacy just looking at them.

'He's not her boyfriend.'

Seriously? You mean they're just friends? That's madness!"

Dancing Feat: One Man's Mission to Dance Like a Colombian

Pay attention

With dance being a physical activity, communication is largely non-verbal. To avoid overstepping the mark, you need to pay attention to the signals you're getting. Whilst I'm sure this can go both ways, I'm more generally talking to the men here. If you put your hand somewhere and your partner removes it, then there was a reason for that. And one might wonder why you had it in her handbag in the first place.

In the reverse role, remember to give off clear signals when a boundary is crossed. Non-verbal communication can be ambiguous at the best of times, and there are definitely those who use dance as a way of getting closer to a partner whilst maintaining the plausible deniability of "we're only dancing". If you're not comfortable with something, make it clear.

Err on the side of caution

All the local people might be dancing quite closely, but this can be in part due to a level of trust that you might not yet share with your own prospective dance partner(s). Being a foreigner can impact on this — whilst you might find that people are intrigued and want to get to know you, they can also be wary, perhaps trying to determine your intention (or even, in some places, considering the impact on their reputation). You're generally best expecting to start further away. Take your time — it's not like there's a fire. And if there is, you shouldn't be dancing anyway. Leave the building by the nearest appropriate exit, go to the assembly point and await further instructions.

Ultimately it's down to you

Only you know what you feel comfortable with. At the start, even dancing with my hand on a partner's back seemed way too close, but over time my personal boundaries became redefined, and I became comfortable dancing more closely.

I asked Vanessa about this situation from a woman's perspective...

"Well, it can be uncomfortable, yes, to dance with someone who is getting too close or whose hands are wandering down the back. Unfortunately, I think I was very passive on this respect. If men were dancing too close, sometimes I was trying to push back, but it was not easy to lose their grip, and I didn't insist. Also, if their hands were wandering down my back (and staying there, still, but in a spot that I would usually not allow) I was pulling the hands back up, and then the guys were just pretending nothing happened, and their hands started going down after a second. A friend who read this question, said that in her case she was always very stern, and if either of these things happened, she would just abandon the guy."

Practice

Practice is optional, but if you want to make the most of your lessons, you should consider it obligatory. The difference it can make to your ability is huge. Even if you're having lessons every day, practice invariably improves your dance skills. You might think (for example) "I've got the footwork nailed already — it doesn't need any practice", but the more you perform a dance move, the more embedded in your 'muscle memory' it will become.

The times I've made most progress have invariably been the times I've been practising, and the exceptions to this have always proved the rule. It does your confidence a world of good, as it means when you go out to a nightclub, you can attack the moves with passion and vigour instead of hesitancy and a sense of 'how did I start that move again?'. It's also the best way to ensure you don't forget all those things you sweated over in the classroom, many of which will completely fade from your memory if you don't keep working at them.

Does dancing in nightclubs count as practice? Definitely. In fact if your aim is to be able to dance socially then this is more than just practising — it's arguably fulfilling the end goal of learning to dance. It's also great experience because you get the chance to dance with different partners with their own idiosyncrasies. If you're leading, then this is when you find out how good you really are, especially if you're leading — a regular practise partner will know from memory what moves you're trying to execute, whereas some new, random partner will only have your signals to go on.

But note that practising in a private space as well as hitting the clubs is still a good idea, as nightclubs are not a good place to be trying out those moves you haven't yet nailed — perhaps the random person you've just asked to dance doesn't actually want their arms wrenched out of their sockets. So there's nothing like dancing away from the spotlight in your own private space for improving your abilities before giving them an airing in public.

It can be hard to get started with practice. A lack of space and/or privacy, not having access to the proper music and even just internal resistance in general can all provide effective obstacles to your doing it. And whilst it's true that if you have the determination to succeed you can potentially make it work anywhere, including partner-less in a backpack-strewn dormitory, this way takes more willpower — a finite resource — making it harder both to get started and to stick at it. So your best bet to getting some practice done is to remove as many obstacles as possible.

"No music to dance to? Fine – I'll just go out and buy some music. No stereo to play it through? Not a problem – I'll play it through my mobile phone. Hotel room too small? Well hey, I'll just dance on the first-floor landing. Should I hear anyone coming I'll just adopt some kind of pensive hand-on-jaw posture.

And so it happens that I finally do it – I finally practise mapalé and champeta – sticking at it despite the odd interruption from cleaning staff, who I leave to draw their own conclusions.

'Look, a man stroking his chin to world music – must be a Guardian reader.'"

Dancing Feat: One Man's Mission to Dance Like a Colombian

Space

If you're normally a dorm dweller, then take the hit and hire a room for the duration of your stay; one big enough that you can execute your moves in. If you can't bear to be away from the social hullabaloo of the hostel, then hire a room there so you get the best of both worlds.

Music

It's easy these days to get the right music. If you have any kind of digital device with a speaker — say a laptop, tablet or smartphone — then you're in the perfect position. You can play it from Youtube, buy tracks or albums from e.g. Amazon or iTunes or stream it from Spotify or its ilk. If you need the Internet to make this work, then make sure that you have it in the place you're staying. If what you're learning is more obscure, like *joropo*, then you should be able to find CDs of it locally.

If you're not sure what music is best, then ask your dance teacher to recommend some tracks that are good for your level and speed. For salsa, it's a good idea to get a track with a voice counting out the beats — "1, 2, 3, 4, 5, 6, 7, 8!" — saving you from the problem of trying to find that elusive '1', and hence lowering the bar yet further.

Partner
Not having a partner will limit what you can effectively practise. I go into how to find one in a later section.

Resistance
If you're struggling with mental resistance to getting started, consider setting your goal ridiculously low, as described by Leo Babauta on Zen Habits (zenhabits.net/habitses). Tell yourself you'll practise for one minute. When you've done one minute, you're officially allowed to stop (although realistically, once you've got started, you'll likely carry on). It's a great way to get a practice habit going, and to get over the hardest part of practice, which is getting started at all.

Remembering Dance Moves

During the lesson, you'll be thinking "I've got this nailed". You'll be full of adrenaline and you'll feel great, and with the sense that this is ingrained and can never be forgotten. But, once again, your brain is playing games with you. As little as a day later, that new move may well have slipped from your mind entirely, or all that remains will be a distant vague outline with none of the details of implementation, making it somewhat unlikely you'll be able to recreate it on the dance floor.

It's understandable that remembering dance steps is difficult. You often cover multiple new moves in a class, and each one contains so many different elements that need to be committed to memory: the positioning and movement of your arms, legs, head and various other body parts; how the movements align to the music; where your weight is; where your partner is meant to be at each moment; and so on. So it really helps to have some method of recording your new moves.

Write it down

Keep a notepad and pen handy on a nearby chair to scribble down the moves as you learn them. If this is not feasible for whatever reason, then make notes immediately afterwards. Unless you're an expert at transcribing dance notation, these written records will almost certainly not be good enough for you to recreate a step from scratch, however many months later, but they should be enough to help trigger off the memory.

Even just having a list of things you need to practise can be a big help. Many steps have names, so ask your teacher what they are. These are very useful as they become part of a lexicon, allowing you to talk about what moves you're having problems with. You can also apply your own if you find a move that reminds you of something in particular.

Film it
You'll need the teacher and/or school's permission for this. This can be a useful reference, but be wary as it's all too easy to fall into the trap of thinking "I've got it all on tape now anyway — I'll practise it some other time". Firstly, you probably won't, and secondly it's a lot harder to recreate moves from watching them on video than you might think, especially with partner dances, when you're trying to work out whose arm goes where.

Use a memory technique
This is especially useful if you're putting together a choreography. One method would be to break the sequence down into chunks, and then label each chunk with something it reminds you of. Then create a story from those chunks. This is my own interpretation of a common technique used by memory experts to remember sequences of cards and the like.

"The resulting story is a little odd. It starts with me changing light bulbs before heading across town on a quest to fix some faulty shoes, before high-fiving a cobbler who broke his leg whilst sweeping the floor. It would make a shit film, but then the point isn't to create a compelling narrative arc – it's to remember a sequence of moves. Besides, I've seen a lot of independent cinema and there's definitely worse stuff out there.

Things are still a touch fitful at first as I have to keep pausing to recall the story, but soon even that disappears: the pasos all just come to me in sequence. My god – the damn thing has worked!"

Dancing Feat: One Man's Mission to Dance Like a Colombian

Take classes with a partner
If you're taking classes with a partner, you have two

working memories instead of one. Between you, you'll likely remember considerably more, and you'll be able to correct each other, too.

Practise as soon as possible

The sooner you practise the moves, the more likely you'll still remember them. Indeed, as previously mentioned, practice is key to improving. After all, most techniques are memory aids rather than memory substitutes. The place you really need that information to be is in your head, ready to recall on the dance floor — pulling out a notepad mid-dance in a nightclub is generally frowned upon — and that can only come through repeated practice.

Finding a Dance Partner

It helps to have a dance partner if you're learning partner dancing.

Yes, that was meant to sound facetious.

Ideally your partner would take classes with you, as there are plenty of good reasons for sharing your learning experience with someone else: you can keep each other motivated, you develop a sense of dance solidarity, it's more enjoyable, it's cheaper, it helps with memory (as previously mentioned) and, most importantly, you've got someone else to blame when it all goes wrong.

But even if they aren't taking classes with you, it's still desirable. After all, whilst a lot of the footwork can be practised on your own, turns are quite something else. And there's only so much a chair or other partner substitute can help.

If you travel in a couple, and your partner is up for dancing, too, then that's ideal. At the very least you'll have something new to argue about. However, if you don't have a ready-made partner, there are still plenty of options for meeting someone suitable:

Hostels
These are great meeting places in general, so there's a good chance you'll be able to find someone else with an interest in learning to dance. They're also cool for finding groups of people to head to a club with.

Social media
You can meet both locals and other travellers this way. Try posting a message on the relevant groups on Couchsurfing, or looking for groups or pages related to dance, dance schools or night clubs on Facebook. You may be able to find someone to help you practise dance in exchange for, say, English-

language practice.

Nightclubs
If you go out and put it about in the local nightclubs, there's a good chance you'll meet someone you can partner up with. The good thing about this approach is that you'll already know whether or not you enjoy dancing with them, first.

Dance school
If you're taking individual classes, your teacher may have individual students at the same level, so ask your teacher to help you — it's generally in their interest for you to enjoy your learning. If you're taking group classes, you'll likely encounter people of all abilities.

It helps to have someone who is at a similar level to yourself, with similar level of motivation, similar goals, and who is planning to stick around for long enough, be they local or fellow visitor. If someone's just partnering you more or less as a favour, or because you convinced them it would a good idea one time over a bottle of aguardiente, maybe they won't see it through.

Even if you don't find a suitable partner, you should go for it and take the classes anyway. Practise what you can on your own — footwork, for example — and then head out at night to get some partner practise. On my own journey through Colombia I was frequently on the move and thus rarely had the luxury of a practise partner. For the most part this worked out fine, though I'm certain that having a regular practice partner would have been better.

"Back at the ranch, I don't find any broomsticks, though I do find a plastic chair in a utility area with a concrete washboard and the smell of drying linen. I have a go dancing with it, whisking it about the tiled floor

61

... It's tiring holding it up ... although less so once I convince the cleaning lady to get off it."

Dancing Feat: One Man's Mission to Dance Like a Colombian

What to Wear

For a dance school, you should wear non-restrictive clothing, such as a t-shirt and shorts or tracksuit bottoms. The exact choice will depend on the climate and weather of the city you're staying in, whether or not they have air con, and how much you enjoy sweating. Whatever the situation, jeans are far from ideal, and will be unbearable if it's hot. Also remember that you won't want to be wearing the same clothes out socially, and what you do wear will need to be washed quite frequently. Unless, of course, you have a profound dislike of people and prefer them to keep their distance from you, in which case rock on.

Regards footwear, you need something that will enable you to feel light and precise on your feet, to execute the occasional turn and, ideally, to avoid crushing the toes of your partner if you mis-step. In other words, clod-hopping walking boots are no good, and the overly grippy nature of a brand new pair of trainers/sneakers means that they might not be ideal. If you're just learning for a bit of fun, then something simple like a pair of pumps / baseball shoes would be a good choice. If you're more serious, then a pair of specialist dance shoes could be a good investment, and most dance schools will either offer them for sale, or be able to tell you where you can pick some up. Bear in mind you'll almost certainly never wear them out at night, and it's another thing to have to travel with, so it's probably not worth it if you only plan to take a week of lessons.

Some folk dances (like *sanjuanero* and cumbia) are danced barefoot, whilst others (like *joropo*) require specialist footwear, which you can generally pick up locally. When I learnt *joropo* for Dancing Feat I needed a pair of *cotizas* (percussive sandals) so I could do the flamenco-like stamping properly — I got a cheap practice pair for a few dollars from a local store. You may need other props too — cumbia, for instance, requires at the very least a special hat (the *sombrero vueltiao*) plus maybe a bundle of candles and a bottle of rum (seriously!), whilst *currulao* needs a special over-sized handkerchief (ideally one you haven't been blowing your nose on). These items will also be available locally, and make great souvenirs.

Out at night, it's all about what suits the occasion and what feels comfortable. In many clubs, casual is the way to go, meaning jeans and a t-shirt for men with, say, a pair of trainers/sneakers or informal shoes (though once again, avoid the clodhoppers). If you're going upmarket, you could wear shoes, but if you're on a long backpacking trip you might find it hard to justify packing them. Styles change, but spray-on jeans are quite common for women, or an unfussy dress. In general, try not to take anything out with you that you don't need as you'll only give yourself something extra to have to look after.

I asked Vanessa what a woman should take to a nightclub...

"I think it would depend on where she was before. If for example, she was working and she needs a bag, she should just bring it and leave it in the cloak room. I think I was usually taking a small bag with my ID, my phone and some money if I went from home. But if, like I said, I was working before, I would just leave my big bag on the seat so it was visible, or I would keep an eye on it all the time. As for high heels, I am not very often using them so in my case I would not use them, unless it were a formal party (a wedding or something like that)."

Lastly comes what is probably the most important point: wear clean clothes and keep good personal hygiene. Dancing with someone dirty and/or smelly is not a pleasant experience, and people will tend to avoid you.

Putting it Out There

The difference between dancing in a school and dancing in a social situation is like the difference between taking driving lessons and ragging a stolen car round a housing estate. Sorry, I meant 'driving on the road unassisted'. So what are your options for putting it out there?

Nightclubs

Clubs are the single best place to go to for dancing, simply because they're in every town and city and the whole point of being in them is to dance and have fun. In fact if you're out with Colombian friends you'll quickly discover that dancing is not optional — it's obligatory. If you're not here to dance, then why are you here?

"Little yellow cars hurtle round the fountain, bottles clank to the ground and people dance around parked-up motorbikes. We're back here again, and I'm talking to some old friends over a soundtrack of trumpets, claves and discordant piano. It's a good night out.

Not everybody is happy with all the conversing I'm doing, however.

'Neil, if you want to chat, go to a café. Here we dance!'"

Dancing Feat: One Man's Mission to Dance Like a Colombian

A lot of clubs play something called *crossover*. This isn't a genre in itself, but just means a mixture of all the urban styles, usually with some regional flavours thrown in. It could be mixed up on a track by track basis, or you might get three or four songs of each genre back-to-back. *Crossover* is a great option if you're learning more than one type of dance, but if you're only learning one there'll be a lot of sitting about looking at your watch and waiting for the next track you can actually dance to. If that's the case, then it might make more sense to head for a specialist venue. Most cities in Colombia have at least one *salsoteca* — (a club that plays only salsa and its related genres). Needless to say, Cali is awash with them. Other venues specialise in reggaeton and similar. I've never seen a merengue or bachata-only club, so *crossover* will likely be your best option for those genres.

Every city and large town has an area called the *zona rosa* (pink zone), which is a concentration of bars and clubs. Larger cities often have several areas where you can head out. The areas, and indeed clubs themselves, can have a very different feel to one another, some being more upmarket and others more studenty, and the atmosphere can vary between the casual and laid back to the more serious. If you go to a club and you don't like the atmosphere, move on and find somewhere you do like.

Clubs generally charge a cover fee to enter, and this is often redeemable at the bar against drinks. There's usually a cloakroom, plus seating round the dance floor so you've got somewhere to park yourself in the brief timeouts from dancing.

Bars

Dancing in bars is also common, indeed the line between bars and clubs can be quite vague at times. In some places, there might not be something you would normally call a dance floor, but that won't stop people dancing — it just means people will dance in what scant spaces they can find. Be prepared to get into elbow fights with chairs and tables. Some places, such as Tertulia la Fuente in Cali take this one step further, with the action spilling out onto the pavement.

Peñas

In the southern Andes, in places like Pasto (and further down into Ecuador), you'll find the bar/club concept known as a *peña* (rock). Popular with a slightly older clientele, they tend to have quite a traditional, rustic feel, and feature a band knocking out covers of well-known classics of different genres along with Andean cumbia and other local flavours.

Street parties

If you're lucky you might come across a street party, commonly known as a *verbena*, and hence your chance to play out that white-rum advert fantasy. They tend to be more common on the coast, probably due to the weather, but you also get them in other places, for instance in Cali during the main festival in December. Also common along the coast is the idea of the *picó* or pickup, which is a stack of speakers and a turntable, usually playing a mix of *vallenato*, reggaeton and *champeta*.

Festivals and concerts

Festivals themselves are usually about watching other people dance, normally down the middle of cordoned-off streets during a parade, or as part of a stage show, but the spirit of the event mean that impromptu dancing often breaks out in the vicinity.

"When I was in the shopping mall, for instance, a middle-aged couple came round the corner to be confronted by the live music. Their reaction was to put their bags down and start dancing with each other – something I've never seen anyone do in Manchester's Trafford Centre. It was a touching moment, the music inspiring spontaneous tenderness between two people who'd probably just come out to buy some bog roll."

Dancing Feat: One Man's Mission to Dance Like a Colombian

Big, multi-band concerts are an essential part of many festivals in Colombia. Exactly what music is playing often depends on the nature of the festival, but whether you're in a big field, or a custom-made stadium, there's invariably plenty of dancing going on in the crowd.

Drinking and Dancing

Although some people do like sitting round tables getting inebriated (especially to *vallenato*, for whatever reason) alcohol is more often an adjunct to the dancing than the point of the evening in itself. People do drink, but you don't tend to see the same level of drunkenness as you do in, say, the United Kingdom, where, for many people, drinking *is* the party.

Regards choice of drinks, spirits are generally favoured over beer, with rum, whisky and the aniseed-flavoured *aguardiente* ('firewater') being the main ones, with specific preference varying across the country. A common way of consuming drinks is to buy a bottle of liquor as a group and then share it out between people in little plastic cups: people go and dance to a few songs, then knock back some liquor as a group, then head back out to the dance floor for more of the real drug.

As a general rule, you should be careful when out drinking. Firstly, drinks do get spiked from time to time, so be cautious about who you accept drinks from, don't leave drinks unattended and try to hang out in a group so you can look out for each other. Also, being drunk puts you in a vulnerable position, so it's worth moderating your intake for that reason alone. Besides, how are you going to dance if you're leathered?

Also be aware of a little thing known colloquially as Ley Zanahoria (Carrot Law) — the legally-enforced closing time of drinking establishments to curb antisocial behaviour.

If you're a non-drinker, you'll find this an easier path to tread in Colombia than in many other countries, precisely because dancing is the evening's central activity for most people. You might get the odd snarky comment from time to time but that's about it. Certainly nothing like as much as if you declare yourself a non-dancer.

Dance and Romance

Dancing with a complete stranger in a nightclub in many countries in the world would rarely be considered as a purely platonic act. In Colombia, however, dancing in itself is generally a neutral act, unless there is something to suggest otherwise. Of course, if you fancy someone else, then dance is a great way to get to know them, but you can't assume that just because you've been offered a dance, or had an offer accepted, the other person is into you. Anyone who is thinking about learning to dance purely as a way of advancing their romantic agenda should bear this in mind.

Personally, I think it's great. It means you can go out with a group of friends, singles and couples, and everyone dances with everyone else, and you all have a really great time. But if dancing doesn't necessarily mean anything on its own, even when done quite saucily (as is normal in some parts of the country), then how can you tell if someone is flirting with you (or indeed flirt with them)?

The answer is that you have to look beyond simply the dancing.

Eye contact is important in dance generally, but extended eye contact and smiling during dancing can indicate interest. Similarly, if someone is repeatedly seeking you out for a dance, or just engaging and laughing with you then they could be into you. Someone trying to talk to you whilst you're dancing can also signify something, though if you're a beginner then this can be like an amateur juggler suddenly being thrown an extra ball.

On a related note, one of the great things about dance is that it gives you a chance to get a feel for the chemistry between yourself and a potential partner. Indeed, someone who you might otherwise overlook can become attractive just by virtue of you sharing a great dance-floor connection. And it can go the other way, too — you found them attractive at first, but now you're dancing together, you find there's no spark.

It's also an opportunity to get a sense of someone's character. Are they funny and playful, or serious and preening? Do they curse and apologise when they make a mistake, or just get on with it? Do they like to dance in an easy and familiar manner, or are they keen to try new things? When you accidentally tread on their immaculately painted toenails, do they laugh and shrug or do they take off one of their shoes and beat you with it?

I asked Vanessa for the woman's perspective. Is it normal for men to try and pick up women via the medium of dance? Is a dance always just a dance?

"Sometimes yes, men can hit on girls when we are dancing in Colombia. But it doesn't mean anything will happen after a night of dancing. From my experience, I can say that a couple of guys (that I didn't know before) asked me twice for my phone number, but nothing else happened. I think it also depends on the situation. For me, most of the time a dance was just a dance, unless there was something building up before with this friend or person that I know. I have an example: my first kiss (I was a little tipsy) happened while dancing with one of my friends. And after that, we started a very short relationship. So, in that case, the dance became something else. Anyway, now I see the dance just as a dance. I think only when I was a teenager I was expecting to find something more than a dance (love, as corny as it sounds) in the dance floor."

How about if you fancy a guy you're dancing with and you want him to know?

"Maybe I would try to make a lot of eye contact, and smile while dancing, and talk, and just have fun. It would be okay to be close (maybe not terribly close, but close enough to feel comfortable), but I would not allow him to do this wandering hands thing."

Finally, if you're already in a relationship, dance can be really cool, too. It can add another facet to the way you both relate, and give you another way of feeling a closeness and a connection with that person. It's also a huge amount of fun, and something that will allow you to indulge in the local culture in a much more shared way than just posing together in photographs. The only issue might be watching your partner dancing with others, something which, if you're out in a group, is hard to avoid as it's perfectly normal for people in a relationship to dance with others. For this reason, it might be worth discussing your personal boundaries with each other first.

Etiquette

Being able to dance is one thing, but you still need to be able to get a dance in the first place, and this is something with its own set of social norms. Given their gender-specific nature, you may not agree with them, but it's worth at least being aware of what they are.

Who does the asking?
It's usually the man who approaches the woman for a dance. But is it okay for a woman to ask a man to dance? I asked Vanessa for her perspective.

"If you are with a group of close friends I think it can be okay to ask a man to dance: in this case I would just propose 'Bailemos' or maybe just signal with my head towards the dance floor, meaning I want to dance with him. But I think I wouldn't dare to ask a complete stranger to dance in the middle of a party because I am a coward. Maybe I would do it if I were drunk, or maybe I would just try to dance near him (but without saying a word) to some dance that doesn't need to be holding hands. I mean, maybe I would quietly dance to some reggaeton or some electronic music. Anyway, I don't think there would be much difference in the way a girl proposes to start dancing."

What do you say?
At first I used to ask *"¿Te gustaría bailar?"* ('Would you like to dance?') or *"¿Quieres bailar conmigo?"* ('Do you want to dance with me?') I suppose I was acting on some image in my head of an English gentleman from a period drama. It turns out that this approach can come across as a bit weak and lacking in confidence, as well as carrying the nuance that the offer is one that requires some thought.

The best way to approach is a lot more direct and simple than that — just smile, offer your hand and say *"¡Bailamos!* [or *¡Bailemos!*]" ('Let's dance!'), or even just offer your hand without saying anything — it's not like your potential partner is going to confuse it for the offer of a handshake, as amusing as that would be. They could still refuse, of course, but at least it shouldn't be because of the way you asked.

Who can you approach?

There are no hard and fast rules about this, but use your common sense (whatever the heck that is). In my own experience, I found the following: If you're out in a group, then you can usually ask any woman in the group, even if attached. If you see a couple on their own, on a date, then it's best to steer clear — it's probably asking for trouble. If you see some women in a group, seemingly unattached, then you can generally go for it. For a mixed group of people you don't know, approach tentatively and be careful not to tread on any toes, figuratively speaking. If you're a man, then it can help to befriend the men first, to reduce the chance of being seen as a threat.

I got an object lesson in approaching people in another group when I was out with some fellow foreigners in Popayán:

"'May I?' asks a big fellow, gesturing towards the German girl. Presumably he thinks we're a couple and he doesn't want to disrespect me by going straight to her.

Flattered as I am by the idea that I have any say in the matter, I accept that I don't, and refer him to the owner of the body in question.

'Ask her.'

She takes his hand and he elegantly whisks her away. Suave, amigo.

Seizing the moment, I immediately head over to the group of people he came from, and approach a man sat with his partner.

'May I?' I say, gesturing towards her.

';Sí!' he says, although 'It depends what you plan to do with her,' would also have been a perfectly reasonable answer."

Dancing Feat: One Man's Mission to Dance Like a Colombian

Social proof

If you're out looking for partners, there are so many factors that come into play regarding the level of success you'll experience. There's the vibe of the club you're in, the people you approach, the way you approach them, and whether or not they think you're just hitting on them (which, of course, you might well be). And then there's social proof.

Social proof is where someone makes a decision based on what they've seen others do. So if everyone is dancing with you, and other people see this, they'll be more likely to dance with you, too. The converse is also true.

From a man's perspective, it can be as simple as this: the first woman turns you down. The second woman sees this and she turns you down, too. Actually, the first woman just needed the bathroom, but it's irrelevant, as a precedent has now been set. I experienced this in a small club in Medellín — I was getting buried under an avalanche of rejections and had to cut my losses and move on to a whole other club. It's worth knowing this, as you could be doing everything right and still be getting turned down purely because people are copying the behaviour of others.

Rejection

Don't take rejection personally. It can burn like heck, but there are a thousand-and-one reasons why someone might say no, and it might have nothing to do with you. Plus, of course, no-one is under any obligation to dance with you. Accept it with good grace and move on. Ironically, if you handle the rejection well, you might find you end up dancing anyway. In one club in Cali, I had a woman tell me 'not now but later'. At the time I figured it was possibly a gentle brush off, and accepted it with a smile. Sometime later that evening, she actively sought me out for a dance.

What about from the woman's perspective? I asked Vanessa if it's okay to say no to a dance.

74

"I think it is okay. I was doing it myself if I was tired of dancing or if didn't like this person in particular. If the guy seemed strange to me, I think I would reject him. I would just tell him 'No, estoy cansada [No, I'm tired]', or maybe a 'No, gracias [No, thanks]'."

For more musings on Colombian dance etiquette and the salsa scene in Cali in general, check out the blog The Dancing Irishman (thedancingirishman.wordpress.com).

Overcoming Fear

There are people in this world who can get up and start dancing with no problems whatsoever. Other people struggle a bit more. Then there are complete dance cowards like me, at least when I first arrived.

"I sit watching a gyrating couple on the dance floor, kidding myself that I'm studying their technique. The longer I leave it, the harder it's going to get. Another ten minutes passes, and the very real danger begins to emerge that I'll leave the club not having attempted a single dance."

Dancing Feat: One Man's Mission to Dance Like a Colombian

What's the worst that can happen? I mean apart from tripping over your feet, grabbing for the curtains, pulling them onto the candles and starting a fire which ultimately burns the whole place down, claiming the lives of scores of people and forcing the owners of the club and everyone who works in it into destitution? But that's only happened to me a couple of times so I honestly wouldn't worry about it.

Anyway, I have some advice for dealing with dance fear, but you're going to be really disappointed with it. Because what you need to do is...

Get up and dance.

Believe me when I tell you this: you cannot think your way onto the dance floor. And the longer you stay sat down, the harder it will get. The only point when things change are when you say "Bollocks to it," and stand up. You'll feel the burn and you'll feel like everyone is watching you (they almost certainly aren't). Now go to someone appropriate and offer your hand. If they accept, lead them to the dance floor. Dance well or badly or excitingly or boringly, but dance. When you're done, revel in the buzz that you just did something that scared you. Fantastic — good for you. If I was there I'd high five you.

The good news is that the first dance is the hardest of the evening, and the second dance comes much more easily. Unfortunately, the next time you head out for the evening you'll be back to square one. Except you won't be; not quite. Because it's like any form of exercise — the more you do it, the easier it gets. The tension, the burn of standing up, the sense of impending doom… you get used to it. In fact, you eventually start to associate those feelings with the buzz to come — overcoming your fears is thrilling and pretty darned addictive.

A few little tips to make life easier for you. Firstly, go out with friends so that you remove the whole dance-approach issue from the equation. Secondly, go and dance as soon as you arrive in the club so you don't have time to think about it, ideally without even sitting down (thought is your enemy, remember, so run with spontaneity and surprise). Finally, learn to recognise when your brain's trying to trick you into taking the easy way out. You'll tell yourself that you're tired, that it doesn't matter, that this isn't a good night for it for a hundred reasons, that you'll do it next time and so on. This isn't the voice of reason. It's the voice of fear. See it for what it is — brain noise — and laugh. Then get up and dance.

Over to You

That's it, we're done.

We've covered a lot of ground here: how to choose a dance genre... how to find and choose a dance school... arranging classes... mind management... the importance of practice... leading and following... language... proximity... remembering all the stuff you've learnt... clothes... alcohol... romance... dealing with your fears... and plenty of other things besides.

Now it's down to you.

Good luck!

Dancing Feat

Dancing Feat is the story of my own triumphs and failures on the dance floor as I journey round Colombia learning how to dance (or, more commonly, doing everything I can to avoid it).

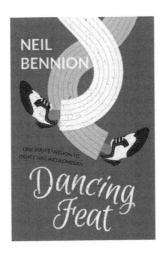

Available now on Amazon (amzn.to/1odeSVE).

"Unmissable! A beacon of inspiration for all wannabe dancers."

"Dancing Feat will spur feelings of both wanderlust and dancerlust"

"Thoroughly recommended if you're interested in dance or Colombia, but also very funny book in its own right"

"Apart from being very funny, I felt really absorbed by the culture and warmth of this fascinating country and its people. It's a great read!"

"Informative, interesting but most of all hilarious."

Mailing List

Want to know when I bring out a new book? Join my mailing list and you'll be among the first to know.

Sign up here:
neilbennion.com/dancereader

Review

Finally, if you enjoyed this book, then do please leave a review on Amazon or Goodreads, even if it's only a few words. That way other people will know this book is worth their time, and I'll get useful feedback.

About the Author

Neil Bennion was born in 1974 in Lancashire, England. He's a writer, traveller and mucker-abouter who left a successful career in IT when he realised he much preferred prancing about in foreign countries to discussing technical scope changes. He blogs about travel, productivity and random other stuff at Wandering Desk (wanderingdesk.com).

Printed in Great Britain
by Amazon.co.uk, Ltd.,
Marston Gate.